Genealogy Simplified

How to Make a Family Tree, Do Ancestry Search, & Trace Family Heritage Like a Genealogist. 75 Free Websites & Resources Included

Cathy C. Schrack

Copyright© 2015 by Cathy C. Schrack

Genealogy Simplified

Copyright© 2015 Cathy C. Schrack

All Rights Reserved.
Warning: The unauthorized reproduction or distribution of this copyrighted work is illegal. No part of this book may be scanned, uploaded or distributed via internet or other means, electronic or print without the author's permission. Criminal copyright infringement without monetary gain is investigated by the FBI and is punishable by up to 5 years in federal prison and a fine of $250,000. (http://www.fbi.gov/ipr/). Please purchase only authorized electronic or print editions and do not participate in or encourage the electronic piracy of copyrighted material.

Publisher: Living Plus Healthy Publishing

ISBN-13: 978-1514808993

ISBN-10: 1514808994

Disclaimer

The Publisher has strived to be as accurate and complete as possible in the creation of this book. While all attempts have been made to verify information provided in this publication, the Publisher assumes no responsibility for errors, omissions, or contrary interpretation of the subject matter herein. Any perceived slights of specific persons, peoples, or organizations are unintentional.

This book is not intended for use as a source of legal, business, accounting or financial advice. All readers are advised to seek services of competent professionals in the legal, business, accounting, and finance fields.

Table of Contents

Introduction 5

Chapter 1: Why Searching For Ancestors 9

Chapter 2: General Overview of Research Process 13

   Becoming a Story Teller, Not a Story Keeper/Collector 19

   Brainstorming & Critical Thinking 20

Chapter 3: Managing Dates 23

Chapter 4: Recording Places 27

Chapter 5: Locating & Evaluating Original Records 31

Chapter 6: Organization 35

Chapter 7: Interviewing Relatives 39

   Before~ 39

   During~ 41

After~ 43

Chapter 8: Deciding What Information is Accurate 45

    Spelling in Genealogy 49

Chapter 9: Death Records 53

    Looking for Records 53
    Alternatives to Death Records 55
    History Clues Contained in Death Records
    59

Chapter 10: Naturalization Records 63

Chapter 11: Social Security Records 67

Chapter 12: Land Records 71

Chapter 13: Maps 75

Chapter 14: Locating Maiden Names 77

Chapter 15: Defining Relationships 81

Chapter 16: Locating Missing People 85

Chapter 17: Adoption in Relation to Family History 89

Chapter 18: Kicking Your Genealogical Search into High Gear 95

   Expanding Your Knowledge in Genealogy 95

   Social Media and the Internet 100

   Family History Myths 102

Chapter 19: Helpful Hints and Tips 107

   Search Tips 107

   Recording Tips 108

   Common Mistakes 110

Chapter 20: Resources and Websites 113

Final Thoughts 131

Introduction

Welcome to *Genealogy Simplified*, a crash course in mapping your family tree from a practical perspective.

Genealogy is the study of your unique family history. It is a personal record of your heritage and ancestors. Such study uncovers where and when your ancestors were born, where they lived, who their children were, who they married and where they belong in relationship to you within your family tree. In case you are wondering just what a family tree is, it's a hierarchy or traceable path through time back to your ancestors, where you originated from.

This book is designed to be utilized as a guide to getting you well under way to tracing your heritage and to help you discover family roots you may not know you had. You will learn the basics of how to begin gathering information, where to look, how to assemble a family tree as well as the do's and do not's about genealogy in a non-invasive understandable way.

When most people hear the term genealogy, they jump to conclusions telling themselves "it's too difficult and complex." But it does not have to be a daunting chore. Tracing your genealogy begins with you. It can be as easy or as difficult as you wish to make it and as brief or as detailed as you desire.

The more information you collect the better the success you will have in discovering your real ancestors. Sometimes ancestors are easily discovered while others may take you long periods of time to discover or for you to decide if you have the correct ancestor or not. The beauty in tracing family lineage is there are no deadlines. You can collect lots of information and take rest periods or collect tidbits continually throughout your lifetime.

Genealogy can be such a fun, exciting and rewarding experience. And sharing the information you gather with friends and family members will give you a feeling like no other. As you make new discoveries, the drive to discover more becomes very intense like adding fuel to a fire, at least this has been my experience.

In the midst of new discoveries comes times of frustration as well. Sometimes it is difficult to uncover new information and often pieces of the puzzle just do not fit together. This can prove frustrating but pressing on and persisting will inevitably lead to new historical information being uncovered and will eventually lead you down the correct path.

It is important to keep in mind as you are venturing into genealogy, that when learning how to go about uncovering members contained within your family, there is no concrete or set way to do so. The tools and principles you will learn in this book can be tailored and utilized in unique ways to meet your own individual needs.

Combining personal flair with your critical thinking skills will help in your genealogic process. It allows you to not only evaluate the viability and reliability of the information you will uncover but will also help to get you thinking outside the box which will ultimately yield more and better information.

This book will walk you step by step in thinking about genealogy, where to begin your searches, building your very own family tree, devising a plan, keeping proper records, analyzing data quality, what to do when you get stuck and most importantly how to have fun learning about where you came from.

Ready to get started? Let's begin!

Chapter 1: Why Searching For Ancestors

You may or may not have asked yourself yet why ancestry is important to you. Perhaps you are merely interested in knowing who make up the members of your distant and ancient family.

Some people use genealogy as a hobby or as a profession. It is fun to learn about family, gather information and uncover mysteries sealed deep in the past. For others genealogy has significant sentimental meaning, maybe there are heirloom possessions that have been passed down through your family that make your history important.

The truth is, ancestry plays a much more important role than meets the eye. While it is comforting to know where you originated from, knowing heritage alone can be powerful and even financially lucrative if lineage can be proven.

There are a multitude of underling reasons exactly why individuals might seek their genealogy. Below are some examples you may be able to relate to. While this list is not a complete comprehensive collection, hopefully it will help to get you thinking about the vast scope of genealogy itself and spark your interest in lifelong learning about your family history.

- **Family Legacy** – Perhaps you have a desire to fulfill or pass on your legacy to future generations.

- **Tracing Medical Aliments** – Maybe you wish to assess your level of risk in certain medical conditions that thrive in families.

- **Historical Studies** – Providing or seeking information about history through studying famous families.

- **Family Traditions** – Preserving knowledge about your ancestors who founded or contributed to traditions contained within your family.

- **Establishing Paternity** – Determining your biological father.

- **Famous People** – You might wish to find out if you are related to any celebrities.

- **Heritage Societies** – Providing documented proof of lineage so you can join a heritage society.

- **Solidifying Family Stories** – Determining whether family stories about your ancestors are true or not.

- **Mapping Family Inheritance** - Determining a genealogical connection for your heirs.

- **Community History** – Determining history of your community by understanding the founders and families who most influenced it.

- **Historical Significance** – Establishing an understanding of your ancestor's involvement in historical and community events.

- **Preserving Family Culture** – Allowing families who have migrated or immigrated to another country the chance to preserve and realize some culture from your original country or origin.

- **Searching For Birth Parents** – Determining your birth parents if you are adopted or attempting to find children whom you have given up for adoption.

- **Religious Reasons** – Satisfying your religious tenets. Mormonism is most well-known for this practice.

- **Reconnecting With Family** – Finding and reconnecting with your living relatives.

Chapter 2: General Overview of Research Process

When beginning your research on family history you should begin by thinking about yourself first. Starting your search for ancestors will be basic and an easy process at first and will become more and more complex as information becomes increasingly scarce or buried in records.

You will want to collect very specific pieces of information for each member of your family tree. Ultimately the information you choose to collect will help you place your genealogical puzzle together and paint a beautiful picture of your unique family history.

Personally I prefer to collect as much information as I can possibly find but not necessarily all at once before I move on to another person in my tree. Once you have some information you can move to other records within your tree and always come back to a previous record to add new information.

You should collect basic information such as

- full name (first middle and last),
- maiden name,
- date of birth,
- place of birth,
- date of death,
- number of marriages,
- date or dates of marriage,
- full names of spouses,
- date or dates of divorce,
- number of children,
- name or names of children and
- names of parents.

The more information you gather will help to give you more pieces of the puzzle to play with and will give you a clearer picture of your true family roots. The reason more pieces of information will help to give you a clearer picture in the long run is due in part to the fact that having more information will help you to rule out poor information and even help you to be certain that you have the correct ancestor.

After all, there are many people who have lived and are still living who share the same and similar names. It is inevitable that at some point in your quest to build your family tree, you will be faced with having to decide between two or more individuals having the same name or information and having to choose the correct ancestor from a group.

Typically this problem will be encountered as information becomes hazy when you are searching for information back a few generations in your lineage. Keeping to the basics will help you avoid problems and confusion so start with yourself first, working back one generation at a time keeping in mind not to become rushed. Often times I see people jump from person to person getting too excited and moving too quickly which just wastes time and makes things messy and unclear.

Record the information about your parents, record the information about your grandparents and talk to your folks about information you are unsure of or do not know. If you are blessed enough to have living grandparents talk to them about their parents or talk to your parents about their grandparents.

Maybe you are the oldest generation still living? That's okay; just record as much information as you know even if you are not terribly certain about its validity. Any little piece of information can be a clue leading to more and more information down the road.

If you have pieces of information say for instance you are working on a date of death but you do not know the exact date, record the year of death as it may lead to further information in the future. If you are unsure of something completely then it is usually best to approximate the information.

For example, if you know you were five when your great grandmother passed away then do the math and come up with an approximate year she died so you have some basis to begin your searches. If you only knew your grandfather by a nickname, document that name as it may be a clue leading to the information you are seeking.

You may or may not be interested in just a few generations of your family tree, which is okay as well. Perhaps you only want to learn about your mother's side of the family. If you have a certain area of focus in your family history go ahead and work on that area until you gain additional interest to work on your father's side, just be sure you are not skipping generations no matter where you are working in your tree.

It is very rare to know the name of a grandparent before knowing the names of the parents. Be certain to collect the information you need in order to solidify each generation. You should use documentation to back up your entries in your family tree.

Do not just assume you have the correct information. The problem in making assumptions is that most of the time improper information gets recorded and lots of time, energy and money gets lost researching the wrong family. This has happened to me. It is a trap that many new people to family history fall into and happens to all of us at some point but staying vigilant in your search and being careful to only record information you know to be true can help alleviate much heartache.

Keeping track of the information you uncover is going to be critical to your long term satisfaction and frustration level as time goes on. When I first began I simply wrote information down on a paper pedigree chart. These charts can be found blank online and can be printed out.

If you are a tactile type of person then this method may suite you well. Just begin filling in those blanks, especially when you are speaking to people and initially gathering information. Once you have some information then you can sort out and decide how you wish to store that information.

Storing information can be done in many ways. You can choose to keep it in handwritten form, you can utilize computerized programs such as family tree maker software and store the information on your computer or since we are now in the information age you can use online sites to enter the information and have it stored remotely.

However you choose to store your information just get it down and document it so it is an orderly easy to access process. Keep in mind when recording names, dates and places; always record women with their maiden names if you know them. The importance of recording maiden names is that they do not change. No matter how many times a woman gets married her maiden name never changes but she can potentially have many surnames.

When searching for information about women contained within your family tree, if you are searching for information on a woman when she was young you will want to be using her maiden name to search. If you are searching for information on a woman in her later years as an adult such as death information you will want to use her married name or names.

Becoming a Story Teller, Not a Story Keeper/Collector

When people think about genealogy the first thing that typically comes to their mind are the names and dates associated with the family tree itself but it is really more than just names and dates. Each unique family tree tells its own story in a very unique way.

Often times it is difficult to get firsthand accounts of stories pertaining to ancestors and in my experience when stories are told they wind up being delivered in a very vague manner. Is it possible that living relatives do not want to tell the gory details of such stories? Is it that they simply just do not remember what they have been told or experienced?

Telling your whole genealogical story is important and it entails more than just a few firsthand accounts alone. Utilizing all of your resources such as the internet, libraries, email, relatives and other tools mentioned in this guide will yield all sorts of different pieces of information helping you to truly get a great picture of who your ancestors really were.

When delivering your story to others be certain to streamline what you are saying, do not cloud the story with too much detail or information, do not focus on the great events of history and remember to include your cousins. Your cousins can be very important as they may know more about your ancestors than you do and they can offer a different perspective or version of family stories as well.

Brainstorming & Critical Thinking

When you get stuck or feel like you are hitting a brick wall, the first step to remember is to go back to the basics. Start with yourself and work back making certain that you do not skip any generations or miss any information.

Oftentimes problems arise like this because there is a mistake that has been made at a very basic level. Have you skipped a step? Are you hitting a road block because you have been researching the wrong person or branch of your tree? Perhaps you have made one or more incorrect assumptions along the way?

Be certain you are keeping detailed records and recording your dates as outlined later in this guide in order to keep track of information you have found. Some of the most common causes for road blocks include:

- not collecting all the information available about an ancestor,

- relying on probable information,

- failure to use the genealogy community as a resource,

- not paying attention to detail, and

- failure to continually educate yourself about up and coming breakthroughs in genealogical research.

The crux of genealogy whether you are working by yourself or with others is to ask yourself a series of questions. What exactly is it you wish to know? Be very clear and specific about what it is you what to know and only focus on one thing at a time.

What information do you know and how do you know it? If you know something simply because it is the way you have always been told without documentation to back it up then you are setting yourself up for failure and serious frustration.

Finally, ask yourself where it is that you could possibly find the information you are seeking? It is very important to keep in mind that if you are not certain about a piece of information and its correctness then do not rely on it to build on. Taking advantage of all learning opportunities and resources available will help you to avoid problems and will make your leaning about genealogy a very pleasant experience.

Chapter 3: Managing Dates

In order to keep your information clear and consistent, dates in genealogy should always be recorded using the two digit day followed by the month abbreviated using the first three letters of the month and then the four digit year.

The way dates are recorded seems to vary vastly depending on the country in which you live. For instance, here in the United States dates are typically recorded month day comma year and in Europe dates are recorded day month year separated by slashes.

Since there are such varying ways of recording dates in the world it is important to have a standardized way to record dates so the two digit day followed by the month abbreviated using the first three letters of the month and then the four digit year is best for genealogical purposes.

I cannot stress to you enough to be certain in recording all years using four digits. Remember, you will be looking at many generations and many centuries in your family tree. Your tree will become extremely frustrating in the future when you have lots of information and you are trying to decide if a year recorded as eighty-seven is indeed nineteen eighty-seven or seventeen eighty-seven.

Here are some additional tips to keep in mind when recording dates. There are standard abbreviations you should use when you are unsure of an exact date. There are many instances where records in the past became skewed as improper information was recorded by hand.

For example, sometimes census records have incorrect names or ages documented. Knowing about these inconsistencies ahead of time can save you a lot of time. And keeping in mind to never rely on just one piece of documentation when solidifying your information will help you to avoid frustration in the future.

When seeking information on a particular event it is best to look for documented records that are closest to that specific event that occurred. When trying to determine a person's accurate age, a census of that person when they are in their eighties is going to be far less accurate than a census taken closer to his or her birth.

Keep in mind that typically at first you will not know the exact information required to produce accurate information. If you are unsure about a piece of information (aged, date, year, etc.) you should place the abbreviation abt. (about) before the information to signify an approximate date or time period.

Other standard ways to document unknown dates and time periods are to use the words before or after. This will help you to narrow down information giving you a better opportunity to increase accuracy of your records in the future.

An example of such is an obituary I discovered on my great grandfather. At that point in time I had not discovered the date of death of my great grandmother yet. The obituary stated that my great grandfather was survived by his wife so I knew she passed away after he did. Instead of not recording anything for her date of death I recorded his date of death so I had a general idea of her death preceded by the word after so I knew she passed away after that date.

Chapter 4: Recording Places

When recording places be sure to always record them from the smallest to the largest. For example, here in the United States you would record places according to city, county, state then country. It will be important to include country on your tree entries because eventually your research will most likely take you to another country where your ancestors originated.

Since many people are now using the Internet to search and store information, your tree has the potential to be viewed and utilized by people in other countries. Therefore, documenting proper country will help to make entries clearer to you as well as others.

If you are unsure of a county within a given territory or state be sure to take a moment and look up the additional information in order to have a complete listing of a place. Having a complete listing will be critical later in your searches.

Sometimes there are more than one town located in the same state that have the same name but are located in different counties. In addition, sometimes county lines change over time and a town located in a county in eighteen fifty can be in an entirely different county in nineteen fifty.

Knowing history of places is extremely important not only to make research easier on yourself but because often times written records are held at a local level so knowing as much information as you can about a particular location the better off you will be.

Once you get to researching very old generations contained in your family tree, properly documented locations become critical; especially if you are at the point of having to personally visit specific locations for additional information or are requesting information by mail.

When organizing information be certain to arrange your information in chronological order according to the person's life for which you are documenting. This will not only help you to be certain that information you collect is accurate, but it also serves almost like a miniature biography of that person's life.

Chapter 5: Locating & Evaluating Original Records

The evidence you collect while searching for information to the puzzle of your family story can be extremely messy. Why is it that the tombstone does not match the draft card? Why is it the death record says something entirely different than that you have grown up knowing?

Information you uncover in genealogy will be conflicting and confusing so locating and evaluating original information is critical. Very rarely does information in genealogy flow smoothly. It is extremely uncommon to find names in the same order, spelled the same way, ages recorded properly, dates exactly correct and correct parents' names listed correctly across all pieces of information.

As you analyze the evidence you uncover in documented records, you should be asking yourself some very specific questions about that information. Keep in mind that as you are searching for information about your family history that you are always documenting and backing up the events you record with evidence.

I like to tell people who are not properly backing themselves up with proof that *"genealogy without documentation is simply mythology."* Just be certain as you are collecting your information that you are sure it is true, correct and you know where the information came from.

Remember, all sources of information are not created equal. The first question you should ask yourself when looking at information is: am I looking at an index or the original record? There is a definite difference between an index and the original record. An index is an overview or someone else's account of what the original record said. Indexes are not always a bad resource but be certain to always use original records whenever possible.

Limiting your use of indexes will help the information you are documenting to be more accurate and reliable in the long run. The closer you can get to an original record, the better. This is because the information has been filtered through less people and there is less chance for error.

Now, even original records are not always completely accurate so do evaluate information you find carefully. When looking at the information you uncover, find out when, where and why the record was created.

I was recently visiting a cemetery to locate the grave of one of my ancestors and was stumped because the tombstone name matched my information but the date of death did not. When I called the cemetery to ask about my findings, they informed me that the stone was placed seventeen years after my ancestor died and the information scribed onto the headstone had indeed been transposed by the person who created it.

With birth records, information is generally reliable as birth records are generally produced at the time of birth without lapse of time and the information is known not assumed or presumed information.

When looking at marriage records, be sure you know whether you are looking at marriage license, a marriage register or return. Caution should be used when looking at military records. Oftentimes this information is accurate but birth years are not always correct in old records, especially those contained in World War One draft records.

When evaluating your evidence, think about how the evidence you have supports or contradicts other information you have already uncovered. Does the evidence you have come from a single source or are there multiple sources?

Furthermore, it is advantageous to find out who provided the information documented, i.e. who the informant is. Think about how strong the evidence you have collected is and address any doubts you may have about such evidence. Are there any holes or lapses of time in your evidence? If so, try to close those gaps by uncovering more reliable documented information.

Chapter 6: Organization

Being organized and keeping track of your information will become increasingly important as you build, uncover and collect more and more records, documents and information on your family history.

Having piles and piles of papers strewn about and things stored in shoeboxes and on your computer in various locations is not only inefficient and disorderly but it is a great way to lose information you have worked so hard to gain. Organizing your data is a great way to revisit what you have and to find things out you may have missed.

The first step in getting organized is to decide where you will keep your information. Will you keep it be online, on your computer in a desktop family tree program, in paper form or some other fashion? Decide which organization method best suits you and keep everything in a centralized, easy to access location.

The most efficient and functional way to store and organize your data is by using a desktop computerized program. These programs have superior functionality allowing you to do more such as publishing your information and use better sourcing tools.

In addition to deciding where your main information will be kept, the following key points will help you to become more orderly:

- Choose how you will store your tree

- Decide where you will be keeping your documents

- Use a simple process to save the document, add the information to your tree, and source the information

- Where will you be keeping back up information?

After selecting where your family tree will be stored and where you will keep your documents you are ready to save your information. Choosing a temporary file in your computer to initially store all information to will be helpful when you are searching because it is easy to just grab a copy of the information dumping it into the temporary file and moving on to the next document.

It is critical to always store your own copy of information and documents as you encounter them because some information is difficult to locate, some information gets lost and other information becomes unavailable. The reason for this is the following:

- you may be unable to find that piece of information when you go back to it again,

- it may not be available any longer from the original source, or

- you may lose access to that information temporarily or indefinitely.

Once you have your information saved in a safe and easily accessible location you are ready to add the information to your family tree. The online site or the desktop software type you are using will drive the actual process of attaching your saved documents to your tree.

When adding documents to your tree, be as descriptive and detailed as you can so when you revisit this information you know exactly what it is and why you attached it. After attaching information to your tree from your temporary file, it is important to permanently save that document to a location outside of the temporary file so you have it for future reference. Be sure to save it in an orderly way.

You can store your information on your hard drive, online, burn it onto a compact disc, the options are endless. I would highly suggest when saving items that you save them according to last name. This way you can consult the file for anyone with that last name and it is an orderly process. And don't forget to make copies.

Getting into the habit of organization will make things easier for you in the future.

Chapter 7: Interviewing Relatives

Before~

It is very important to prepare meticulously before you interview relatives, so you can ask the proper questions in an efficient manner in order to get the most out of your time invested.

Before conducting any interviews you should make a written list of whom you could possibly interview. Begin your list with the oldest living family members and work forward being careful not to overlook anyone who can contribute valuable information.

Be sure to include family members from both sides of your family regardless of how close they may or may not be to one or both sides of the family. This is the perfect opportunity to rekindle and reconnect with people in the family you have not spoken to in long periods of time.

Do not forget about members of the family you may have not met before. Think outside your immediate family and even go beyond your extended family circle so you can attempt to interview as many people as you can.

Think about how you want to conduct your interviews. Do you wish to conduct them in an informal or formal setting? Informal interviews can be just as easy as formal ones but can yield very different types of information.

Also, do you wish to conduct your interviews one on one or in groups? Keep in mind that interviewing someone one on one will uncover different information versus interviewing multiple people together at one time. Multiple people can spark off of each other helping to further the accuracy of information. One-on-one interviews should be used for more intimate discussion.

Before you interview you will want to think about how and where you will be conducting the interview. Personal face to face interviews are nice; however sometimes in person interviews are not always realistic. Using the telephone, mail and email are all great options to utilize if a personal face to face interview is not possible.

Make a decision about how you will record the information you will be gathering during your interviews. Do you wish to hand write responses, record them on an audio device or even on video? Handwritten notes can help to improve details as you can interject small bits of information here and there as they come up.

The biggest thing you should do prior to conducting your interview is to have a pre-prepared specific set of questions. Using lists of questions will help your interview to flow properly and smoothly. Before conducting any interview you should have a theme or focus as to what it is you wish to lean.

During~

If you have done your interview preparation correctly then the interview itself becomes the easy part. When conducting an interview, if you are recording using audio or video be sure to ask the permission of you subject first. Do not automatically assume everyone will be okay with being recorded.

Most of your interviews will be conducted on older generations so take special note and be sensitive to the comfort level and any medical or health related conditions of your interviewee. Queue in to the best times of the day to conduct your interview. Perhaps the person you interview has better recollection of past event in the morning? Be sure also not to conduct marathon interviews allowing your subject bathroom and meal breaks, even conducting multiple smaller interviews can be appropriate.

During interviews myths or family stories may surface. If your subject states anything you know to be untrue or false do not attempt to dispel rumors or offer your version of the story during the interview. This sort of behavior will only lead to premature conclusion of your interview obstructing your ability to extrapolate all the information that person has to offer. Confrontation will always impede your ability to gather crucial information.

Allow the person you are interviewing to lead the interview if possible. At the conclusion of your interview ask permission to follow up and schedule a future meeting if necessary. Do not procrastinate gathering information and be sure to thank your family member for helping you.

After~

If you made a recording of your interview on audio or video, make a copy or two immediately after the interview and store the additional copies in an entirely different location. Accidents and natural disasters happen so making a copy or two will help to preserve your information and hard work.

Immediately after your interview you should also spend some time extracting pertinent family historical information. Do not waste time while your memory is still fresh. Get those thoughts documented and into your family tree.

Additionally, within a day or two of your interview take a few moments to write a handwritten thank you card or letter to your family member whom you interviewed, especially if they are distant and not someone you know very well.

Chapter 8: Deciding What Information is Accurate

It is very common in genealogy, especially for those new to genealogy to get excited and overlook critical information even accepting pieces of information that may or may not be accurate. It is extremely important to learn how to analyze information from an accuracy standpoint and learn how to think about what it is the information is trying to tell you.

In genealogy there is a standard established called the genealogical proof standard. Like any other entity this standard is a prescribed method or set of rules to follow established by the board of professional genealogists to help you compile the most accurate information available for your own individual family history story.

The Proof Standard states that you should:

- Conduct a reasonably exhaustive search

- State complete and accurate source citations

- Analyze and correlate the collected information properly

- Resolve any conflicting evidence or unanswered questions

- State a soundly reasoned, coherently written conclusion

It is important to keep in mind that this standard is an established set of guidelines for professional genealogists. You may or may not wish to adhere to its strict standards but it is important for you to know the general theory behind genealogical research.

When analyzing the information in which you will uncover you will want to be thinking about many things in order to make a decision about the validity of it. Just because you uncover several documents which state the same information does not necessarily mean that the information is true and correct.

Think about death records for instance. If you are looking at a death certificate, you are trying to establish this person's date of birth and said person died at the age of eighty. The informant who gave the information contained on the death certificate most likely knew the person well. That person at least knew the details surrounding the death but was most likely not present at that individual's birth. If there is a conflict of information about this person's date of birth, using the death certificate information alone to render your decision would be a mistake making that person's date of birth unreliable.

There are many points in human history where errors can and have occurred relating to the correct and accurate documentation of information. You should also keep in mind when analyzing information that most of the information you will encounter has been handwritten, copied and rewritten many times. There are plenty of opportunities through time where mistakes could and have been made. Sorting these errors out can be daunting and extremely frustrating at times.

After you have conducted a reasonably exhaustive search for information, you have analyzed that information and you have thought about what that information means you should be to a point where the information begins to fit together nicely or perhaps there are many conflicts to be resolved.

If there is a lot of conflicting evidence after your search and thoughts then the information is probably not correct. In this case you would want to continue searching for more information to find the correct answer to your question. Finding as much documentation as you can is critical to proper decision making in genealogy. Finding a birth record in this instance would be the ideal situation to solving this problem.

Keep in mind that the answer to your genealogical questions is not necessarily the number of documents you uncover that state the same information. It is entirely possible for a single source to be correct even when there are five other sources which agree with one another consistently that are not correct. The best rule of thumb to use when you cannot locate the answer you are seeking is to keep searching and digging for more information and documents until you are confident that the information is true and correct.

Spelling in Genealogy

It is important to keep in mind that when you are researching you should be aware that spelling over time has had very little uniformity merely because most of your ancient ancestors probably did not know how to read, write or spell properly.

In fact, there were no technical spelling or writing rules instituted in language until about 1775. Even then most people who lived in that time period did not have access to those rules through education so writing and grammar was far from how we know it today.

Typically in the past people did not fill out forms and write their own information. Someone else listened and transcribed for them oftentimes writing what was heard and not necessarily correctly. Up until recently when we began filing out government documents ourselves, spelling and names just were not a priority.

There are many reasons for spelling errors and changes in spelling and it will be crucial for you to keep these reasons in mind during your searching in order to locate, extract and utilize the information in which you are seeking.

In regards to spelling the most important thing to keep in mind is not to get hung up on spelling or a certain way thereof. The quickest way to create a road block is a closed mind about spelling something one specific way especially when it comes to names.

Be creative in your searching. Sometimes it is useful to physically write down every way you can possibly dream up to spell something you are searching for and institute all those spellings in your searches in order to uncover a whole new multitude of possibilities for information.

Another way to attempt uncovering spelling variations aside of writing is to speak out loud the word you are looking at and see if perhaps you can derive other ways of spelling it based on what you hear or how someone else sounds saying it.

Different branches of families tend to spell their family name in different ways. Even siblings can often spell their family names differently as well. Occasionally results will be different because of a translation variation rather than merely a spelling variation. It is quite possible that your ancestors could have used a name that translates across languages rather than using the same spelling alone.

Simply stay vigilant when searching. When you are sifting through search results look at everything that logically makes sense. Even queuing into something off the wall can prove beneficial at times.

Chapter 9: Death Records

Looking for Records

The more information you know about vital records the more successful you will be in finding and accessing such records. Death records are important for providing quite a bit of valuable information and can help to solidify whom you have found and confirm members of your family tree.

Death records are a very peculiar subject in and of themselves as some records do not even exist or are not published. Each state or territory has their own rules, regulations and locations that govern death records. Modern day death records are routinely held at the state level in most if not in all areas today in the United States. However, in some areas death records were held at a county level instead of with the state making them even more difficult to access.

If you are searching for a particular death record, the first step to do is to find out if the record actually exists. It may be completely possible that the death record in which you are searching for does not even exist. This is because the death information in which you are searching was not recorded, was not properly recorded or perhaps the information is held in a different capacity.

The best references you can utilize to obtain information about death records are two published guidebooks. The guidebooks are titled "**The Source**" and "**The Red Book**," both of which are referenced in the end of this book so you can easily find them. These books provide detailed information as to what, when and how death records are managed according to the state.

Once you have searched and found out if the death record you are looking for even exists, the next step is know where to find the record in which you are seeking. There are databases located online where you may be able to locate the records you are looking for. If you are unable to find the information in a database you may be able to locate indexes or other archives available such as **Cyndi's list**.

Cyndi's list is a website located at www.cyndislist.com and is a resource for genealogic data and you will likely find the information found on that site to be useful.

If your efforts are not fruitful or you prefer not to use the Internet to search for information then state libraries or state archives are the places to look. In some states the state library and state archive are different organizations and in others they are the same. Be certain to check both places as each may yield different and enlightening information.

The alternative to contacting state offices for death information is contacting the entity where the original record is held to obtain a copy by mail or in person.

Alternatives to Death Records

If you cannot locate a death record or one simply does not exist do not panic. There are alternatives to aid you in getting the information you are seeking. The following are suggestions of places to look if state or government offices are not an option in obtaining death information on your ancestors.

Obituaries~

One of the most obvious alternatives to a death record is an obituary. Obituaries have traditionally been run in newspapers for several centuries to announce death information to the general public. Not all deaths were or are coupled with an obituary but it was a very popular way to announce deaths in the early nineteen hundreds and before.

Libraries are a great resource to utilize when searching for obituaries. If you are having trouble locating an obituary for one of your ancestors, consider contacting the library where that ancestor lived.

Many libraries have local historic newspapers for their area on microfilm and you might have success locating the obituary you are seeking at a local level. If you are unable to visit the library personally, do not worry. Oftentimes libraries will employ a research librarian who can and will locate the information you are seeking for you for free. Sometimes for a small fee the research librarian will find the information and mail to you a copy of his or her findings as well.

Cemetery and Tombstone Records~

Tombstone and cemetery records are not the same. One of the largest free, volunteer-run databases for tombstones is **Find a Grave**. This is an online catalog located at www.findagrave.com and is an excellent resource for tombstone photos. If you are lucky, additional information may be recorded along with the photo which can aid your search.

Cemetery records are the paperwork associated with the purchase of a plot or section of land. Not all cemeteries have such records available and not all of them are willing to share such records, but it is a great resource to check into if you are seeking additional information or cannot locate death record information pertaining to your ancestor.

Probate Records~

Another great resource for additional information especially when searching for ancestors who lived in the seventeen and eighteen hundreds are probate records. If your ancestor had a legal written will this is where you will find that information.

Probate records can sometimes help to narrow down dates of death, define other relationships and pinpoint locations of people contained within the will. Historical societies oftentimes retain these types of records.

Guardianship Records~

Another document often prepared around the same time as the probate records are guardianship papers. These papers were documents prepared to ensure the continued and proper care of minor children and/or dependent adults.

Keep in mind that depending on which time period you are searching, guardianship papers can be found for a child or children that had a deceased father but still had a living mother. In early times such children were still considered to be orphaned. Guardianship documents basically legally stated who was to step in to care for the children and their mother after the death of the father.

The best place to locate guardianship records are county courthouses or county and state archives.

Other Records~

Estate records are another small piece of information that can be utilized if death record information is not available. If your ancestor owned property then an estate record was generally documented and these records are usually held by archives and libraries. Estate records deal with the management and sale of property upon death outside of probate records.

Hospitals and funeral homes in the area where you think your ancestor lived can sometimes yield good information also. Funeral homes not connected with a cemetery will generally have copies of death certificates and obituaries if they exist.

History Clues Contained in Death Records

Death certificates contain death related information but are so much more than simply a recorded date of death. Such certificates can contain a wealth of valuable information such as:

- A person's name
- Where they died
- Cause of death

- Attributing causes to the cause of death
- How long that person was attended to by a doctor
- If there was an autopsy performed or not

Sometimes death certificates also include information about:

- Occupation
- Marital information
- Spouses' names
- Parents' names
- Parents' birth places
- Information as to where the body was removed to
- Whether the person was buried or cremated
- Funeral director information
- Funeral home details and much, much more

Every death certificate form is slightly different depending on the time period in which it was made, the county it was made and the state involved.

When you are analyzing a death record, be certain to pay special attention to the informant listed. The informant is the person who provided the information contained within the death certificate. The informant listed could be a spouse, a child, a sibling or other person who knew the deceased person well. Sometimes just knowing the name of the informant can lead you to more information in your searches.

Something else to keep in mind about informants is that an informant may not have known all the correct information about the person who died in which they were reporting. It is possible for misinformation to be listed on death certificates if the informant was mistaken.

Chapter 10: Naturalization Records

Naturalization is a very difficult and complicated process. It is the legal process involved in becoming a citizen. Since naturalization is and was a legal process it involved lots of paperwork thus creating a record or paper trail.

In the process of naturalization there was a wait period, the period of time from immigration to the time naturalization could commence and again from the time of commencement to the time a petition was filed to be naturalized.

The initial paperwork filed is called the declaration of intent or "first papers." The petition was later filed when said person was ready to become a citizen are typically referred to as "second papers."

When searching for records on naturalization it is important to obtain not only the certificate of naturalization for the person in whom you are researching but the declaration of intent and the petition that the person filed as well. The declaration of intent and the petition contain all the information about the person, their family and their immigration so having both will greatly improve your knowledge about that person.

In 1862 it was deemed that any men who served in the military were allowed to naturalize without filing a declaration of intent alleviating the wait period and of course making the paper trail less.

From 1795 through 1906 the law stated a two-year continuous residence waiting period in the United States before you could submit the declaration of intent and apply to become a citizen. And there was an additional three-year waiting period from the time the declaration of intent was filed until the petition could be filed. So the process of naturalization was known to be a five-year minimum process.

Prior to 1906 the process of naturalization was handled by local courts so if you are seeking records on an ancestor prior to 1906 you will want to look into old court records on a local level to where your ancestor resided. In 1906 naturalization became a federal process and records are retained in the national archive.

Prior to 1922 women and children had derivative citizen status. This means that when the husband became naturalized as a citizen so did his wife and children. Keep in mind when looking for naturalization records, women and under aged children between 1906 and 1922 of naturalized husbands and fathers will have no written records of naturalization.

In 1922 the law changed and women were able to naturalize for themselves. They did not automatically become citizens due to their husband's citizenship and had to file their own naturalization paperwork.

The first thing to do when you are trying to locate naturalization paperwork is to narrow down the time period of when your ancestor immigrated and naturalized. Not all immigrants naturalized within the standard five year window of time. Some people waited longer periods of time and others never naturalized.

Between 1890 and 1930 it is approximated that twenty five percent of the population was not naturalized and those individuals had been in the country longer than five years. It is entirely possible for you to locate multiple declarations of intent due to misunderstandings in laws and relocating to different areas in the country.

Chapter 11: Social Security Records

Social security records are yet another place to find great information about an ancestor especially if you are having difficulty finding information on that individual or you are trying to resolve conflicts within the information or records you have already discovered.

The social security death index contains information about individuals whom have contributed to or drawn from social security in their lifetime. The index contains the following information:

- Name of individual

- Date of birth

- Date of death

- Place and year the social security number we issued

- Last place of residence

- Last benefit received

Not all social security records will have a complete listing of all the above referenced items, but it is to your benefit to check the listing for your ancestors to see if perhaps additional information you do not already have is contained within that ancestor's social security record.

Some records will have an entry listed about the last benefit received. This benefit is typically one that was paid to a qualifying survivor such as a spouse or a child. If a record you encounter has no recorded last benefit entry but has a last place of residence listed then it is safe to assume that said ancestor had no eligible survivors whom could claim the social security benefit and the last known address where benefits were being paid is listed.

If you are analyzing a record which states no last place of residence and no last benefit received, this could very well mean that someone is still collecting benefits from the deceased person's social security administration account or that person died before receiving any benefits and had no dependents who could claim those benefits.

Social security record information is generally not available for recent deaths in order to protect the privacy of living individuals of the family. It may be advantageous to order a copy of your ancestor's social security application itself for a small fee directly from the social security administration in order to obtain this valuable information.

Chapter 12: Land Records

Land records are yet another piece of information, a tool that can be extremely useful in discovering information about your family history. You might be wondering why land records should be used in genealogy. Using any and all records available to you will help to maximize your ability to ensure accurate information and will help you extrapolate as much information about your family history as possible.

Land records are used to tie people to a certain place and time. While this may seem like a redundant task because census records are also used to tie people to a specific time and place, what if census records are not available in your search?

Land records can help when you have exhausted other resources for information and they often go back to further periods in time not encompassed in other available records.

Another great use for land records is to help sort out people who had the same names that lived in the same places.

Kinship can also be established using land records and can really aid your ability to link relationships in your family history. Not just familial relationships can be established using land records; they can be utilized to help you learn information about the community as well.

Understanding people who married into the family, people who did business with the family and people involved in the lives of your ancestors will help to tell your family history story and further your research.

Understanding the geography of where your ancestors resided can also help to explain why they did some of the things you will discover. Such records can help to explain why your ancestor got married where they did, why they lived where they lived and why they may have moved. They will also help you to solidify your conclusions about your family history links.

There are many types of land records available. Each record has its own specific type of information according to the land type for which it was intended. The following list is a variety of land record types:

- Deeds – Property transfer document from one person to another usually containing information about all parties involved in a transaction and sometimes it will provide the relationships of said parties as well as information about the transfer itself.

- Tax Records – Specifically land taxes

- Estate Records

- Homestead Applications – Applications for homestead establishment

- Probate records

- Private Land Claims

- Plot Maps – Detailed documents about property boundary information

- Survey Systems

- Bounty Land Warrants – Property deeded for military service

Land records are sometimes critical in family history research as they are often the only records available in the early 1800's and late 1700's research. They can help you understand the geography of where your ancestors lived, the relationships they had with others, who they lived near, who lived around them and how land use or ownership changed over time.

Chapter 13: Maps

Maps are sometimes very useful in family history for many reasons. They can make the journey of discovering information more interesting in your quest for answers but more importantly maps provide additional information which can help to connect two pieces of unrelated information or solve conflicts in your information.

You should use maps because over time land borders, county lines, street names and numbering and population expansion into new areas have made some of the places once inhabited by your ancestors all but unrecognizable.

Geographical features and land marks may have determined where your ancestors went to town and perhaps left records. In urban areas, historical maps can help you to pin down ward numbers and enumeration districts which can help you to narrow down your search in other records. Maps may also illustrate where churches and cemeteries were located in relationship with your ancestor's home.

Collections of historical maps can be found in many places including libraries, historical societies, and places online. Even local county or state archives have such maps. One of the surprising features of historical maps is that they are often coupled with illustrations of some towns giving you an idea of what your ancestors towns looked like.

Chapter 14: Locating Maiden Names

When you begin thinking about how to uncover the maiden names of the women in your family history, the first thing that should come to mind is marriage records. Marriage records are the easiest way to discover maiden names. Just make sure you do not overlook all the possible types of marriage records available.

Be certain when looking for marriage records you investigate marriage applications for licenses, certificates themselves, wedding announcements, wedding engagement announcements, bonds, banns, civil registrations and divorce records.

When investigating marriage records make sure to thoroughly scour the information and fully understand it. If you are unsure how to interpret a record take the time to research just what it is you are looking at. Sometimes a woman listed a previously married name as her last name instead of a maiden name so be sure you are looking over closely to discover the true maiden name of each woman in your family history.

Cemeteries, burial grounds, tombstones and adjacent plots are also great sources in uncovering maiden names of women. Just because a tombstone lists the married name of a woman does not mean you cannot find her maiden name there.

Look at the burial records, queue into adjacent plots where your ancestors are buried paying extra special attention to names of people buried nearby.

Pay particular attention to the cemetery name as well, sometimes family names have a relation to the name of the cemetery itself.

Census records are another great place to uncover clues to maiden names. You should get a full run of all census records available on all your ancestors in both married and maiden names. Scour the censuses and look for brothers, sisters or other people listed in the census who lived in the same household which could shed light on maiden names of others in that same home.

There are other notable places where maiden names can also be discovered as well, those include:

- Land records, deeds and transfers of property

- Church records ~ Membership and christening records often list maiden names. Look for other church members listed in records as well; perhaps other members of the same congregation are family members who carried the family name. Church records are also a great place for information before the census began in eighteen sixty.

- Probate records and wills

- Historic newspapers ~ Women often were referred to as misses plus their husbands name in newspapers. Such newspapers often published information about small engagements even dinner parties listing names of attendees.

- Birth and death records ~ You should seek information on not only the woman you are interested in but focus also on her children as well. Piecing the puzzle together can often lead to the uncovering of maiden names.

- Military records ~ Typically you probably think of men when thinking about military records but when seeking such records in relation to women you should be thinking about the pension records specifically.

- Naming patterns ~ Pay special attention to naming patterns contained in the family. Be sure you look at first and middle names also. It was very common in early times to use maiden names as middle names for children but was not always a rule.

Chapter 15: Defining Relationships

You may have heard the term your third cousin once removed or you may have encountered relationships listed on probate or land records that you do not exactly understand. Definitions of relationship have changed over time so understanding the true meaning of such relationships is critical to your understanding about your family history and just how certain individuals fit into your family tree.

Understanding relationships can become messy fairly quickly once you begin thinking about adding in step relationships and adopted family members. Step children are simply the children of a spouse by a former marriage who have not been adopted by the step parent. A step parent is defined as the current husband or wife of your mother or father who is not your biological parent. Step brothers or step sisters are the children of your mother or fathers current marriage.

In-laws are defined at the family of your spouse or the spouse of your children. In-law used to be defined as a relationship that could be legally defined so it is important to keep in mind that when looking at old records the term in-law does not necessarily mean related by marriage.

When trying to define cousins the first place to start is to determine who the common ancestor is. If your common ancestor is a parent then you are siblings. If your common ancestor is a grandparent then you are first cousins. If your common ancestor is a great grandparent then you are second cousins. If your common ancestor is a great great-grandparent then you are third cousins and so on.

The term removed can make understanding relationships very confusing. This term refers to relationships when the two people you are comparing are in different generations. Things surrounding cousins begins to get super dicey very quickly because the term cousin has not always meant the same thing over time.

Cousin used to mean a close relative historically. Today some people define friends as part of their family calling them brothers, sisters and cousins in spite of any blood or genetic relationship.

The terms aunt, uncle, niece and nephew get confusing also because they have not always meant the same things over time either. The terms junior or senior do not always signify a relationship between a father and son as well.

Sometimes there are cousins who have the same name living in the same community who will go by junior or senior in order to have a differentiation within their own community.

The idea of genealogy is to help you identify structure and to help you identify relationships and such terms are used to help you in this process but sometimes they only cause more confusion than they do helping out.

Chapter 16: Locating Missing People

It is likely in your searching that at some point you will encounter missing people. Generally these missing people are people located on census records but can be missing on other records.

As you approach census searching there are a few things to keep in mind. You should be asking yourself a few simple questions so you can assess the validity of the recorded information. What was the census taker told? Who told the census taker the information?

As a rule of thumb if a census taker visited a home three times and found nobody home all three times then they would often rely on neighbors to get census information which was not always accurate information. Also, there were certain periods of time where it was not acceptable to be from specific countries such as Ireland or Germany so people did not give that information or they lied about their descent by Americanizing their names.

How did the census taker hear what they were being told? Perhaps that taker was interviewing someone who had a strong accent and did not record the information spoken to them accurately.

It is also important to keep in mind when looking for missing people in family history records to know what type of document you are viewing. Is it an original copy or an index of a record? If it is an index you are looking at the transcriber might have made a mistake when typing the index. Not all census takers had legible handwriting so it is completely possible that information could have been lost or mistakes could have been made during the indexing process.

Do not automatically jump to conclusions and assume that your family was somehow missed in a particular census because the chances of that are very seldom. Keep digging for information as persistence will pay off in the long run.

When searching for missing people in your family history, keep the following list in mind when looking for new information:

- On your first search do not search for anything exact

- Search for specific information in databases

- Narrow your search results by modifying and adjusting key search words

- Search for all members of the family not just one

- Search for all people of the same last name living in a specific location

- Try searching by first name with no last name

- Search with no name but use other information such as birth or death dates

- Search city directories to determine exactly where the missing person in which you are searching may have lived

- Look for neighbors of previous censuses

- Browse the entire community where you think your ancestor may have lived

Do not allow yourself to get discouraged when searching for missing people either on a census record or on any other records. I have mentioned this and I will say it again, do not give up looking for unknown information. Your persistence will pay off in the long run.

Chapter 17: Adoption in Relation to Family History

Adoption may seem like a rare and unique niche of genealogy that only affects some people but that is not generally the case at all. The reality is that you will most likely be affected by adoption at some point during your genealogic research. It is not really all that uncommon.

When the industrial revolution began it is estimated that seven out of every one hundred births were illegitimate. Often times those illegitimate births were children given up for adoption or raised by a family member. The challenges of adoption associated with genealogy are figuring out why the adoption occurred and where to properly place those adoptions within your family tree.

In relation to history the term orphan was commonly used for children who lost just one parent and not necessarily both. Orphans could be a result of a death of either parent. If the mother died in a family it was common for the father to allow another member of the family to raise the children so he could work.

Generally speaking, adoptions in history were not formal processes as we see in the world today. It was very common for adoptions in the past to be very informal and simply a verbal agreement. Regardless whether an adoption was formal or informal there is still a possibility that a paper trail exists to support such history therefore employing your investigative abilities is very important when looking into adoptions in general.

Adoptions before 1850

When searching for adoptions before this time period you should look for information in a different way than later adoptions. Things you should consider are:

- Adoptions were often informal
- Scour probate records carefully
- Look for apprenticeship records
- Check guardianship records

- Look into poor law records (community supported children)
- Look for bastardy documents and illegitimacy records

Adoptions from 1850-1950

Before closed adoption laws became widespread in the United States, information about adoptions were assembled and stored differently. Keep in mind that this time period is well known for informal adoptions. You will still want to look into:

- Where did the adoption occur?
- Orphan trains (1853-1929)
- Look for records such as census, guardianship and probate dockets.

Charitable institutions and organizations in the area where your ancestor lived that may have kept records on such adoptions. Such records usually contain things like:

- When the child arrived?
- Who dropped that child off?

- If the child had siblings
- When the child left the institution and where they went?

Adoptions after 1917

In 1917 there was law passed that started what we now know as the modern adoption era or modern adoption laws. After about thirty years all states had passed laws providing for such adoptions like closed adoptions.

The laws were primarily established to deal with the shame associated with illegitimacy or children born out of wedlock mostly to protect the birth mother rather than keeping the information sealed from the child.

When searching for adoption records in this time period the following should be addressed:

- Where did the adoption occur?
- Is the adoptee over eighteen years of age?
- Petition the court in the county where the adoption occurred for information

- Register with state and national reunion registries (even if the adoptee is deceased)

- Look into hospital records

After you have made an exhaustive search and found records pertaining to adoptions, it is important to document both the adoptive parents as well as the biological parents in your family history. This will help to keep things flowing smoothly when you go back over your information or if someone else is trying to follow your findings.

Chapter 18: Kicking Your Genealogical Search into High Gear

Whether you are just beginning or you have had a lot of experience in genealogy there comes a point where knowing just a little more information could aid you greatly in making your family history connections stronger. The best way to do this is reading and educating yourself in order to learn more about genealogy in general and information about your own individual needs.

Expanding Your Knowledge in Genealogy

In addition to reading, attending lectures and events about genealogy can help you to increase your knowledge base drastically. There are many places online where you can find resources that we will discuss later.

Home study courses are available and in some circumstances there are professional genealogists to consult.

Local and state genealogical societies often have educational programs and presentations that you may find useful. You do not necessarily have to be a member of your local genealogical society in order to attend their meetings or educational presentations but being a member may save you money on registration fees associated with their class offerings.

In order to locate your local genealogical society contact the Federation of Genealogical Societies, there you will find a listing of all societies in your area in which you may be able to further your genealogical knowledge.

Another place to look for more information on a local level is a family history center. These centers are run by the Latter Day Saints Church and can offer additional information about events available to you on a local level.

Attending national genealogy conferences will also help to further your knowledge and offer many amenities associated with genealogy in general. The five main genealogy conferences held each year are:

- The Roots Tech Conference

- National Genealogy Society Annual Conference

- Federation of Genealogic Societies Annual Conference

- International Association of Jewish Genealogical Societies Conference

- Southern California Genealogic Society Jamboree

Educational classes offered at such conferences tend to be very focused and structured toward specific topics even as specific as focusing on certain record sets, specific collections, things to look for in specific locations and much more. One great aspect of attending these conferences is that it allows you to network with other people who share the same interest. Oftentimes just speaking with others who share the same interest can help to spark your mind and give you new ways to approach your genealogical research.

In order to prepare and get the most out of a conference you should take a good look at the class listings beforehand. Select which classes you wish to attend. There will most likely be several classes you wish to attend at the same time block so deciding before the day of the conference can really help to alleviate confusion and wasted time.

Once you have made your class selections do not just think about what it is you wish to get out of the class. Make sets of specific questions you wish to be answered for each lecture you will be attending. Check to see if the class or lecture has a Facebook group or event online and join that group. If you have been reading posts and interacting with the same group of people for several months prior to the conference you will be more likely to maximize what you get out of the lecture itself.

When you get to a conference, actively participate in the lectures you attend. Get to the class early to get a good seat so you can be more engaged in the lecture. Take lots of notes during the lecture. Generally the lecturer will provide a syllabus about the talk on the day of or prior to the lecture. Talk to people at the lecture as it is important to get acquainted with people sitting around you and learn about things they are hoping to learn at the lecture.

Lastly, be certain all the questions on your list were answered during the lecture. If they were not be sure to ask because there are probably other people in the audience with that same question as well.

Another way to really become deeply serious about your learning of genealogy is to study to become a certified genealogist. This certification is a boarded portfolio which is extremely difficult to achieve as there are less than three hundred certified genealogists in the United States today.

The board for certification of genealogists was established in 1964. It looks at various areas of genealogy skills and requires different materials for each certification category. Although no specific program of education is required for this certification, rigorous knowledge, skills and education is essential to a successful completion.

The certification is a seven step process which must be completed over a period of one year.

1. Planning (up to one month in duration)

2. Active research and biographical information (up to one month in duration)

3. Active research and documenting work (up to one month in duration)

4. Active research and client report (up to one month in duration)

5. Case study (up to two months in duration)

6. Kinship determination project (up to three months in duration)

7. Review, revision and submission (up to three months in duration)

The bottom line here is that learning is an evolving process. The more you educate yourself about genealogy the more you will be successful in uncovering what it is you need to know or want to know. Education will help you to form better questions about what exactly it is that you are seeking and will also help in breaking through periods of dead ends.

Social Media and the Internet

The Internet has undoubtedly crept its way into all of our lives whether you wanted it to or not. With the information age booming and technology coming at you from every angle, I'm sure you have been exposed to a few mainstays such as Facebook, blogs and Twitter.

Leveraging the information you find online will not only help you to understand and learn about the world around you but it can really help you to understand the world as it was in historic times long ago. In addition to learning while using the Internet, it is a great place to connect and possibly grow your family tree by discovering more information in a quick and efficient manner.

Blogging about family history is one way to share and receive information about genealogy and family history. A blog is basically an online diary in which you can write, post photos and share things using the Internet which comes up in search results when people enter search terms that match what you have blogged about.

There are several platforms online in which you can use to blog. Some online blogs are free to use while others cost monthly fees. Blogging is also a great way to reconnect with distant family members you may have lost contact with over time.

Facebook is a large online social media platform that has taken the Internet by storm. It seems anyone and everyone has used and uses Facebook regularly online. Facebook is a resource that can be very useful in genealogy. It can be used to share genealogical information, receive information, connect with family members and start discussions.

Facebook is a great place to create pages relating to ancestors in which others can click like and connect with you. The benefit of using Facebook pages is that anyone who does a Google search online that includes a word or words of your Facebook page in their search will see your page in the results.

Facebook has extremely high rankings in all search engines online so it is a wonderful avenue to begin connecting with people all over the world who have similar interests.

Family History Myths

Family history myths get circulated frequently from one person to another, from one generation to the next and can become perpetuated or morphed. They may make good stories but simply are not always true. Some myths are common and others are more particular to your family. Getting to the bottom of family stories is important in uncovering the truth. After all the truth is what you should be seeking in compiling your family history.

One very common myth in family history is name changes occurring at Ellis Island. It is important to understand that passenger lists were created by captains of ships before leaving their origin and not after arriving at Ellis Island. Ellis Island began operating in 1892 so any ancestor who predates 1892 did not come through Ellis Island.

For the period of immigration in which Ellis Island operated there was a process and laws governing such process which created paperwork. Such documents were often created by a clerk in that individual's home country who knew and spoke the same language.

The employees of the ships generally checked the immigration documents very closely at boarding time because when ships arrived at Ellis Island the documents were scrutinized. Improper documentation was a quick ticket to being sent back to the originating country.

Most commonly name changes did not occur at Ellis Island itself. In general, names became Americanized by the immigrants themselves over the first few years after immigration.

There are lots of myths surrounding Native American family history. When investigating information about Native American stories, keep in mind that Native American culture did not have princesses. If you have been told a story about ancestors who had contact with a Native American princess, that story is most likely not true.

At one point in history the term "Native American Princess" was a racial slur used to refer to an inter-racial relationship not necessarily involving a Native American at all. It is also common for people to analyze photos noting high cheek bones and dark hair and jump to conclusions that said person in the photo is Native American.

You should not fall into this trap. Heritage cannot be possibly proven through photographic evidence. There are many nationalities of people who resemble the characteristics of Native Americans so be sure you do not begin making assumptions based on photos.

Another myth that surfaces often relates to family coats of arms. There is no such thing as a family coat of arms. Coats of arms were assigned to individuals and they are still to this day governed in Europe with a strict process by heraldry registries. Upon the death of someone who has a coat of arms, their heir can apply for permission to display that coat of arms. It is possible for a family who has lots of sons to have many coats of arms because they are assigned to individuals and not to families.

When analyzing family stories you should follow a process in order to help prove or disprove them based on their merits and not solely based on assumption. The following list is a good rule of thumb you can follow to help in your evaluation.

- Collect all versions of the story.

- Where did you hear the story?

- Talk with family members separately as well as together.

- Probe for details by asking questions.

- Think outside of the immediate family box.

- Think about yourself if you find out a story you believe is not true.

- What can you immediately prove or disprove?

- What parts of the story do you know to be true?

- Think about how the story could have changed over time.

- Document the story & your findings about it.

- Do not be afraid to tell the true story once you discover it.

Chapter 19: Helpful Hints and Tips

Search Tips

When searching for information on family history it is important to learn ways to search efficiently in a smart manner in order to uncover more information, save time and even money. When diving into searching for information on your ancestor it is very easy to get carried away and only search using limited information.

Keep in mind that when searching for information, searching for the most detailed information you know will help provide a more narrow set of results to weed through. Not all search results will be of the ancestor of whom you are seeking and not all records you find on your ancestor will yield all the same information or all correct information.

Sometimes it is advantageous not to search exact names in case records exist where the name is abbreviated or that ancestor had a nickname that he or she went by.

If you are having trouble locating exactly where an ancestor was living at a given point in time, it is a good idea to look into adjacent states in which they lived especially if that ancestor lived near the border of a state.

Recording Tips

When documenting your family history it is extremely important to write those things down. Writing your family history down will not only help to improve your writing skills but you will also learn and retain more of the information you uncover.

When locating documents you should carefully read that document and understand it but you should also transcribe that document according to your understanding of it. Transcribing the information you read will again help you to retain that information but it also forces you to read every detail in that document allowing less error in overlooking important pieces of information.

As you are assembling your transcriptions, be sure to put them in chronological order so the information flows well is orderly. Organization is crucial as you will be referring back to this information from time to time.

Recording your information in chronological order gives you a working document that will make it easy to glance back at the last recorded entry so you know what piece of information you need to be looking to add next. In addition to transcribing documents it is important to tell the story behind your document if you know additional information.

Sometimes when recording information it is helpful to make a written family timeline or map in order to properly visualize the chain of events for your family history. Do not be afraid to take some time and construct a simple timeline if you are a visual person as this will help you to better digest and understand your information.

Recording family stories is also another important thing to do because as people age memories are not always the same, pieces get lost, things get forgotten and getting those stories down on paper will help to retain accuracy in the future. Recording personal history helps to preserve this same rule of thumb and that should be documented accordingly as well.

It is a good idea to getting into the habit of making notes about your findings regardless if you have documentation to back them up. For example, let's say that from the early 1800's information you have been analyzing, you discover that a substantial portion of your ancestors moved from a particular area. It might be advantageous to begin researching historical events and natural disasters for that given area and noting those things in your timeline accordingly.

Collecting mementoes and writing about those is another great idea to add personal touch to your genealogical collection. Such mementoes like photos, family recipes, special documents, as well as audio and video collections each carry a story. Making a written document about each memento will help to preserve history for many generations to come.

Common Mistakes

Mistakes happen in genealogy and there seem to be a lot of them. Do not feel badly if you have made some of these mistakes. Just try to keep them in mind in your continued searching.

The following are the top five mistakes commonly made when researching genealogy:

- Jumping to conclusions without documentation to back your view up

- Assuming your family name is only spelled one way

- Researching the wrong family

- Failing to document your sources

- Relying on the family trees of other people

The following are additional mistakes you should be watching out for and are a bit less common in genealogy research.

- Not recording what you find or recording the information in multiple places

- Ignoring your ancestors' brothers and sisters

- Overlooking maiden names of female ancestors

- Recording women with married names rather than their maiden names

- Assuming you are related to a famous person or anyone with the same last name

- Skipping a generation

Be sure to stay vigilant when researching your genealogy so you do not waste your valuable time. Be certain you are verifying information and gathering documentation which back up your findings.

Chapter 20: Resources and Websites

The following is a listing of resources, websites and books. They are listed in no particular order to aid you in your genealogy research, family history discoveries and personal discovery.

www.census.gov– This site is a government site run by the Unites States Census Bureau. Here you can locate information collected in censuses and much more.

www.awesomegenealogy.com– General tips, databases, directories, tools and helpful information for beginning your genealogical research.

www.bcgcertification.org– Information on becoming a certified genealogist. Offers what the proof standard is, things to study and the steps involved in gaining your certification.

https://familysearch.org– This site is a good starting place for searching for genealogical information offering family tree building help, learning information, blogs and the opportunity to connect with others about common topics.

http://genealogy.about.com/cs/free_genealogy/a/free_sites.htm-- 101 ways to research your family tree for free, alternatives to pay-for-use genealogy sites on the internet. There are lots of great ideas on this site to save you money on your genealogy quest.

www.newberry.org– Research library located in Chicago offering extensive information on genealogy and historical records.

www.lds.org– The official site for the Church of Jesus Christ of Latter-day Saints. This site has many links and information on family history and genealogy including how to get in contact with your local Family History Center.

http://emptynestancestry.com/-- Information and links associated with genealogy in general including tips, hints and advice regarding genealogical search and researching an extensive family tree.

www.legalgenealogist.com– Great blog conducted by an attorney who is a certified genealogist. This site gives a great legal perspective to genealogy.

http://agraveinterest.blogspot.com/-- This is a great blog about cemeteries, genealogy and history containing photos, information and interviews about researching in cemeteries in general.

www.ffhs.org.uk– The Federation of Family History Societies is an educational charity developed to assist people interested in family history, genealogy and heraldry.

www.apgn.org– The Association of Professional Genealogists site offering information about genealogy, ethics, conferences and hiring a professional genealogist.

www.genealogyintime.com– This online magazine offers articles and how to guides, contains listings of new genealogy records and the very popular genealogy this week column.

http://expertgenealogy.com/pro/-- This website lists independent companies and individuals who provide genealogy related products and services including professional genealogical research. These services are listed in directories organized by geographic and research specialties.

http://generousgenealogist.com– A site for great information run by a community of volunteers who agree to provide free genealogy research and assistance, as an act of kindness, to "those in need." They are a vibrant, vital and growing community teaching and helping each other in the best methods and traditions of the genealogists of today, yesterday and hopefully tomorrow.

www.ancestorsatrest.com– This site offers free searches of death records such as coffin plates, death cards, funeral cards, wills, church records, family bibles, cenotaphs and tombstone inscriptions. You can also find links to other death records like cemeteries, vital stats, and obituaries here.

www.adoptiondatabase.org– A resource for adoptees, birth parents and siblings, other birth family and adoptive family members in the process of searching for missing links.

www.ngsgenealogy.org– National Genealogy Society leads and educates the community and its members in tracing family history, new innovative breakthroughs in genealogy and national conferences.

www.lds.org/locations/temple-square-family-history-library-- The Family History Library located in Utah is the largest of its kind anywhere in the world. This library has the most extensive collection of genealogical information anywhere.

www.familyhistoryzone.com– A great place for beginners offering the ultimate dimension in genealogy and family history. This site provides information and tips on all sorts of records including birth records, marriage records, death records, census, passenger lists, military records, probate, newspapers directories and more.

www.blm.gov– General information on land patents offering many databases about land records.

www.archives.com– Information on finding ancestry and historical records quickly and simply offering extensive searches for images, newspapers, vital records, and more.

http://usgenweb.org– This site is a volunteer run, non-commercially funded website offering free information and resources on genealogy topics categorized by state.

www.onlinefamilynetwork.org– This website has been established to give family history researchers a complete one-stop website to conduct research and to network with one another.

https://sites.google.com/site/freeancestryforbeginners/--This is a Google listing offering a comprehensive list of free ancestry resources and how to use them.

www.cemeteryregistry.us– This website is a registry of United States based cemeteries and their locations.

www.historybuff.com– This page is maintained by a nonprofit organization devoted to providing FREE primary source material for students, teachers, and history buffs. The focus is primarily on how news of major and not so major events in American history was reported in newspapers of the time. In addition, there is information about the technology used to produce newspapers over the past 400 years. The latest addition is panoramas of historic sites in America.

www.afamilytreeguide-chicago.info– A beginner's guide to tracing your family tree. This guide stems from a seven part lecture series providing guidance, tips and links for genealogical research.

www.myheritage.com– Offering information on general genealogy topics, heritage searches, family tree building tools, message boards and more.

www.thinkgenealogy.com/map-- Neat information mapping out the process of genealogical research offering a great approach to conducting your methods of gathering information.

www.genealogybranches.com– Good website that has a bunch of record related materials such as census, military, naturalization and vital record information.

www.50states.com– This site has a complete and comprehensive listing of newspapers in the United States categorized by state.

www.ancestry.com– A wonderful place to find in depth information of family history and build your own family tree online.

www.theoldentimes.com– Great listing of historical newspapers including news, obituaries, marriage and birth notices, advertising and an index of names.

www.genealogy.com– Offering family history searches, family tree building tools and basic things to do when searching for information related to genealogy.

www.familytreemagazine.com– Great resource for basic information, genealogy 101, genealogy essentials, monthly podcasts, forums, frequently asked questions, online genealogy classes, downloadable forms and how to go about tracing your family tree.

http://genealogy.about.com/-- Information on a variety of genealogy topics, how to's and tips on getting started and continuing your searches for good information. Also offers webinars and general information on genealogy.

www.cyndislist.com– This site is a great resource of general and specific genealogy websites you can visit. This list is extremely comprehensive and can offer many options if you hit a road block in your information searches.

www.vitalrecordsus.com– Great resource in locating vital records throughout the United States and more.

www.adopteeforum.com– Forum offering members of the adoption triad a place where they can openly voice experiences, concerns and feelings surrounding adoption.

http://genealogytipoftheday.blogspot.com/-- Great place to visit daily for new tips and motivation in continuing with your research.

http://geneabloggers.com/genealogy-free/-- This site does a great job of explaining why genealogy research is not always free and what things you need to do to prepare yourself for things that will cost you money. Also offers general information about genealogy and hosts many blogs that may be of interest to you.

www.genealogyarticles.com– Good general site containing lots of genealogy related topics and articles.

www.fold3.com– This is an online repository for original historical documents, combined with the ability for users to make comments, annotations, and upload their own documents. The focus of the site is to be a comprehensive collection of United States military records. Some areas of the website are free to use, while others can be freely searched and then viewed with a paid subscription.

www.rootstech.org– This site is information all about the RootsTech national genealogical conference. Here you will discover how to register; you can view the schedule of classes and discover a whole new world relating to genealogy in general.

www.findmypast.com– Great site offering information, tools help you understand, analyze, manage, and interpret your results, sources for records including overseas documents, family tree building tools and much more.

www.e-referencedesk.com/resources/state-history-timeline-- This site provides a chronological timeline chart of important events and dates in the history of each of the fifty US States. Browse key events in each states history chronological from 1600's to 2000's, with developments in politics, presidents, popular, Native American, planetary, technology, and culture. Also, access the United States early history, state facts, state history firsts, and famous people.

www.jgsgb.org– This site is the home of the Jewish Genealogical Society of Boston, a non-profit organization dedicated to the growth, study and exchange of ideas and information among people interested in Jewish genealogical research and family history.

www.fgs.org– The Federation of Genealogical Societies offers lots of information on a multitude of genealogical topics, it acts as a link between genealogical societies helping them to grow and is famous for their annual conference.

www.family-genealogy.com– This website allows you to build and organize a precise family history and a reliable family tree that can be shared with family and friends.

www.uscis.gov– The United States Citizen and Immigration Service offers lots of information on citizenship and immigration. Thy have an extensive section on genealogy and helpful information relating to citizenship.

www.rootsweb.ancestry.com– One of the oldest and largest free genealogical communities. An award winning genealogical resource with searchable databases, free web information and more.

www.ahgp.org– The American History and Genealogy Project offers a large collection of resources in discovering American and family history. You will find lots of independent sites devoted to genealogy here.

www.alhn.org– The American Local History Network Inc. is a nonprofit public benefit corporation whose mission is to serve as a central point of entry to independent historical and genealogical sites on the Internet.

www.genealogytrails.com– This site is a volunteer project, transcribing genealogical and historical records in the United States for the free use of all researchers.

www.ssa.gov/history/history.html-- Information on social security and historical aspects of the social security administration.

www.archives.gov/research/genealogy/index.html-- The National Archives site listing many resources for genealogists and hobbyists looking for information on family history.

www.scopesys.com/anyday-- This site is a really neat and fun place to plug in dates and get a listing of historical events which occurred on that given date.

www.ages-online.com– This is a great place to build your family tree online. The site offers lots of ways to personalize your tree while keeping things simple and manageable.

www.aaslh.org– The American Association for State and Local History offers support to those who preserve and interpret state and local history. They offer many educational opportunities to learn about historical times.

www.museumstuff.com/index.php?p=topic&qw=Historical%20Societies– Comprehensive listing of historical societies and their addresses located throughout the United States.

www.scgsgenealogy.com– This site is the Southern California Genealogical Society's website where they pride themselves on their research library and offer information on family history projects, information about genealogy in general, record databases and they have information about their annual Southern California Jamboree conference.

www.historicpathways.com– Site maintained by renowned genealogist Elizabeth Shown Mills. She packs the site with great articles, community studies, historiography, theory, case studies, professional issues, research reports, great book listings, links to valued sites and information about herself.

Evidence Explained: Citing History Sources from Artifacts to Cyberspace by Elizabeth Shown Mills, Publication Date: June 30, 2007 ISBN-10: 0806317817 ISBN-13: 978-0806317816 Evidence Explained is the definitive guide to the citation and analysis of historical sources. It begins with a simple question: Why do we invest so much of our energy into the citation of sources? Followed by the intriguing answer: Because all sources are not created equal. As a citation guide, Evidence Explained is built on this simple question and answer.

The Researcher's Guide to American Genealogy by Val D. Greenwood Published in 2000, ISBN-10: 0806316217 ISBN-13: 978-0806316215 This book is a wonderful book arguably the best book ever written on American genealogy. This book has become a classic and is utilized by many colleges and universities, designed to answer practically all the needs of researchers.

Mastering Genealogical Proof by Thomas W. Jones–Mastering Genealogical Proof guides readers in acquiring genealogical skills transcending chronological, ethnic, geopolitical, and religious boundaries. The book aims to help researchers, students, and new family historians reconstruct relationships and lives of people they cannot see.

Professional Genealogy: A Manual for Researchers, Writers, Editors, Lecturers, and Librarians by Elizabeth Shown Mills, ed. ISBN: 9780806316482 Professional Genealogy is a manual by professionals for everyone serious about genealogy. For family historians who want to do their own study, reliably, it describes the standards. For hobbyists, attorneys, and medical scientists who seek professional researchers, it's a consumer guide that defines quality and facilitates choices. For librarians who struggle to help a whole new class of patrons, it provides a bridge to the methods, sources, and minutiae of "history, up-close and personal." For established genealogical professionals, it offers benchmarks by which they can advance their skills and places their businesses on sounder footing. And for all those who dream of turning a fascinating hobby into a successful career, Professional Genealogy details the preparation and the processes.

Red Book: American State, County & Town Sources Edited by Alice Eichholz Publication Date: June 1, 2004 ISBN-10: 1593311664 ISBN-13: 978-1593311667 No scholarly reference library is complete without a copy of Ancestry's Red Book. You will find both general and specific information essential to researchers of American records providing county and town listings within the same overall state-by-state organization. Whether you are looking for your ancestors in the northeastern states, the South, the West, or somewhere in the middle, Red Book has information on records and holdings for every county in the United States, as well as excellent maps from renowned mapmaker William Dollarhide.

The Source: A Guidebook of American Genealogy Edited by Loretto Dennis Szucs and Sandra Hargreaves Luebking, Publication Date: June 1, 2006 ISBN-10: 1593312776 ISBN-13: 978-1593312770 Often referred to as the genealogist's bible this book is intended as a handbook and a guide to selecting, locating, and using appropriate primary and secondary resources, The Source also functions as an instructional tool for novice genealogists and a refresher course for experienced researchers.

Our family history by editors of Readers digest, publication date: October 25, 1999 ISBN-10: 0762102322 ISBN-13: 978-0762102327 this book is a great place to keep hand written documentation of family tree records. This is a readily available book offering lots of fun options and a very nice layout.

The Complete Idiot's Guide to Genealogy by Christine Rose and Kay Germain Ingalls Published January 3, 2006 ISBN-10: 1592574300 This book is wonderfully user friendly offering opportunities to understand the craft of genealogy, exploration of your roots, perform online research and begin to discover identity.

Final Thoughts

Genealogy is so much fun. It is exciting and extremely addicting once you begin to uncover new information. Just keep in mind that you do not know what you don't know. There is always so much more to learn so make an effort to learn as you go.

Many opportunities exist for self-education and to connect with others like you. New sources of information can surface or you may discover something you missed on a record at any point in time. Do not get discouraged when your search becomes frustrating and you seem to hit a brick wall or road block.

When you think you have done everything you can possibly do to find what you are seeking just take a deep breath and try to look again with refreshed eyes. Ask yourself what you already know about the particular situation or person. Think about information you want to know and discover. Brainstorm alternative places you believe you can look to find new information about what you are seeking and be humble.

When investigating your family history, be sure to keep an open mind about everything you uncover, read and collect. Do not get stuck in one mode of thinking about what you know and what you do not know or what you believe about your family history. This will slow your progress and even prevent you from gaining valuable information discoveries.

Hopefully, with your drive combined with the information provided in this book you can get off to a great start searching, uncovering and building your own family tree. Keep in mind that genealogy and history are things that you can continue to learn and build upon for a lifetime and the information offered here is by no means everything you could possibly know about genealogy.

The more ambitious and aggressive you are in your searching for information, the more fruitful your efforts will be. Pace yourself and take breaks. Some people constantly search for information about genealogy at a slow steady pace and others use an intermittent approach where they search hard for several days and then take several days break in between. Whatever approach you deem best for yourself be sure to have fun, stay vigilant and share your findings with friends and family. You never know who might take an interest in genealogy and want to help in your search.

Best of luck in all your searching!

Printed in Great Britain
by Amazon